Therapeutic Stories

Principles & Techniques of Story Therapy for Children

By Violet Razegh Panah

Translated by Abtin Jodat

PUBLISHING

Title: Therapeutic Stories; Principles & Techniques of Story Therapy for Children
Category: Psychology, Parenting, Non-fiction
Author: Violet Razegh Panah
Translated and Edited by: Abtin Jodat
Layout and Cover Design: Abtin Jodat

Published by V BOOK PUBLISHING
ISBN 978-1-4467-5824-3

Intentionally left blank.

Contents

Intentionally left blank.

Foreword

The telling of tales is an ancestral art that binds generations in a common human tapestry. Stories hold an alchemical power to illuminate, elevate and heal. As we gather round the fire to share our lived experience through imagining otherwise, we kindle flames of insight that cast light on timeless truths.

As an influential contribution to the emerging field of therapeutic storytelling, this book elucidates the profound power of narrative to heal psyche and spirit. Drawing upon extensive clinical experience, the author outlines effective techniques for employing storytelling to nurture creativity, self-understanding and emotional intelligence in children facing diverse challenges.

Spanning various insightful points, the text analyzes common parenting approaches that, despite good intentions, often inadvertently suppress young imaginations. From over-structuring and repetitive routines, to overemphasis on outcomes and arbitrary social judgments, such missteps discourage the risk-taking and self-exploration vital for creative flowering.

Seeking solutions, the author delves deeply into storytelling's therapeutic potential. Masterful tales build linguistic facility, curiosity, focus, retention and cognitive skills. Most profoundly, as fictional characters model compassion and courage, they spur self-reflection, empathy and resilience in the child. Stories provide a safe harbor to encounter life's realities through the adventure of imaginative worlds.

Yet nurturing creativity requires artistry. The consummate storyteller intuits the child's interests and abilities to craft emotionally compelling narratives. Cliffhangers, suspenseful pacing, participatory prompts and multi-sensory details sustain engagement. Still, technical mastery alone does not suffice. Channeling love and insight, the healer's essence catalyzes the therapy; unconditional acceptance kindles the child's inner light.

Enriched by case studies, the text examines therapeutic storytelling for conditions from learning disabilities to depression, aggression to PTSD. Tailored tales empower and restore, gently reshaping limiting mindsets. Even significantly troubled children discover hope and meaning as fictional heroes overcome similar trials. Though trauma casts shadows, narrative's light reveals resurgent possibilities.

In the first chapter, we critically analyze philosophies and best practices for promoting healthy childhood development. A child's journey from dependence to self-discovery is discussed, highlighting the need for parents to cultivate wisdom and compassion through alternating periods of tranquility and tumult.

The second chapter provides an evidence-based framework for leveraging therapeutic storytelling to help children overcome psychological, developmental, and behavioral challenges. Drawing on clinical research, we delineate how skilled storytelling practitioners can externalize inner conflicts, reframe limiting narratives, and build resilience through metaphor, catharsis, and modeling self-efficacy.

Specific techniques examined include reshaping negative thought patterns, conquering inner demons through allegory, fostering social participation for shy children, and customizing interventions based on disabilities. The therapeutic storytelling process aims to ignite children's agency to rewrite constricting narratives that hamper growth.

In essence, this work evaluates storytelling as a tool to light up the human condition and nurture children's wellbeing. A developmental perspective is applied to provide actionable guidance on parenting philosophies and healing-centered narrative practices. Synthesizing modern psychology with timeless wisdom, this writing brings to light the storyteller's art of instilling self-belief through archetypal metaphors and role modeling. The overarching goal is cultivating empathy, curiosity, and compassion in children so their unique gifts may benefit society.

Further, by making these practices accessible beyond the source language, I hope this translation would enrich the diversity of perspectives applied towards nurturing children's growth. Parents, educators, counselors, and scholars across the globe now have access to an expanded toolkit for fostering empathy, curiosity, resilience, and benevolence. May such compassionate principles proliferate, helping all youths unlock their creative potentials to bless the world.

Abtin Jodat, August of 2023
Toronto, Canada

Chapter One
Our Children, Life's Jewels

Cultivating the Budding Spirit on Childhood's Journey

Opening

As a new soul enters this world, eyes still adjusting to unfamiliar light, we watch in wonder at the genesis of a unique being who will journey through childhood's alternating landscapes of storm and calm. Though bearing the markings of ancestors, each child is a fresh spirit whose petals have yet to unfold. Our vital task as parents is to tend this budding flower, discerning the contours of its emerging temperament and providing the nourishing rain that will enable it to flourish.

In this chapter, we will walk together through the seasons of childhood, appreciating each phase of growth and equipping ourselves to guide little feet along the winding road ahead. Like a gently flowing stream, we will explore childhood's meanderings from the infant's first breaths to the lively currents of imagination, self-assertion and social initiation that begin swirling around ages three to five. As the child's energies surge and recede in alternating moods of cooperation and rebellion through the ages of six to eight, we will consider how to meet these oscillations with wisdom, empathy and perspective.

Just as cultivating orchards requires adapting to each tree's needs - pruning here, fertilizing there, coddling one sapling while urging another to toughness - we must discern each child's unique strengths and shepherd their authentic flourishing. We will reflect on establishing early foundations of literacy and numeracy, fostering cognitive growth through exposure to nature's splendor and mankind's diverse creations. As social awareness dawns around five years old, we will seize this chance to instill self-reflection and consideration for others.

While every child delights in fantasy, guiding play towards cooperation and away from violence sows seeds of compassion. As their curiosity combusts through ceaseless questioning, we have the privilege of nurturing an inquisitive spirit. Our task is to expose children to varied terrains yet avoid forcing conformity, cultivating instead their innate wisdom and accountability. Just as gardeners shape promising growth while allowing each flower's true colors to unfold, we can guide children to become anchored oak trees offering shelter, nourishment and beauty to all.

After long anticipation, the precious new arrival makes its fatigued yet eager entrance, breathing its first breaths in an unfamiliar realm. Though bearing the genetic imprint of ancestors, each child is a unique being, with distinct traits that will gradually unfold.

A parent's vital role is to nurture the flowering of this spirit. The infant may appear plain or fair, loud or quiet, calm or colicky. Yet all are born in innocence, with equal dignity. By attending closely, parents come to

Some babies focus intently when nursing, while others readily distract. Some sleep and eat on a schedule, others resist routine. Some adapt to disruption, others protest change. Multiple temperaments emerge, from sensitive to easygoing, from stubborn to cooperative.

By observing closely during the first year, patterns become discernible. Better to gently discourage undesired behaviors now than permit them to become ingrained. Set loving yet firm limits, neither yelling in anger nor inflicting physical punishment. Withdraw attention, not affection, when unwanted behaviors arise. Stand resolute today to avoid exhausting power-struggles tomorrow.

From ages two to three, self-assertion intensifies, as the child's universe revolves around his immediate wants. Expect resistance and boundless questioning during this absorption in self. Meet each objection with simple, reasoned answers, as their minds cannot yet process nuance.

Throughout these foundational years, parents' unconditional love scaffolds the young soul. Children blossom best when offered warmth, wisdom and judicious structure by caretakers mindful of their still ripening spirits.

Around one year of age, an infant discovers the delight of vocalizing. Gradually they learn to mimic simple words and sounds. As their mental concepts expand, objects and people gain familiar labels - «kitty» and «doggy» stand for whole categories. Educational toys assist cognitive growth at this stage.

Toddlers revel in exploring their burgeoning physicality - everything is alive and tossing items to the floor brings endless amusement! They begin to identify body parts when prompted. Following simple commands emerges, though expectations must align with their capacities. Music, especially classics, greatly aids neural development, even more so when paired with movement.

As abstract thinking progresses, pretend play arises, along with curiosity about the surrounding world. Answering their ceaseless questions through engaging joint storybook reading enables the blossoming of literacy and reasoning abilities. Books become trusted companions, teaching about people, nature and life's possibilities.

Nearing three years old, self-awareness expands - children recognize themselves in mirrors and begin mimicking others. Artistic expression unfurls through drawing. Puzzles captivate their concentrating minds. Imaginary friends inhabit fantastical internal dramas.

During these cognitively fertile years, loving patience and responding to each unique child's needs, while exposing them to nature's beauty, books' wisdom and music's inspiration enables their innate potential to come to full flower. The seeds planted now yield the fruits that the future will harvest.

Cultivating a Love of Reading

Establishing reading routines plants the seeds for lifelong literacy. Sitting together engrossed in a book's world, taking turns turning pages, the child learns books are treasures holding wonders. Though their attention may initially waver, they persist in sharing story-time's joys.

Model articulating words clearly and precisely. Let them explore switching lights on and off, mastering cause and effect. Avoid comparisons that could instill unhealthy pride. Children see parents as all-powerful in early years. Alterations to their appearance can seem frightening, though familiarity will dispel this.

Around three, possessions gain value, prized toys tagged along everywhere. Never lie, even in white, for trust in parents' omniscience is absolute. Some kids experience normal developmental challenges like temporary stuttering that resolve naturally. Meet anger with calm patience, not alarm. Left-handedness should be encouraged, not "corrected."

Laying foundations of literacy, curiosity, and resilience enables children to bloom. Patiently nurture their true nature, watering with wisdom, light, and love.

A young mind blossoms through exploration, not correction. Behold their journey with wonder, not judgment. Speech flows from thought, not sound - perceive errors as growing pains, not flaws requiring remedy. Calm patience is the gardener that nurtures vocabulary to fruitfulness.

Around the tender age of two, interest stirs in the body's functions. Allow infants to tune into their own natural rhythms, free from shame or restriction. Harsh potty training sows seeds of anxiety that distort digestive health. Far worse is the lasting scarring upon the psyche - despair dims inner light as anger and obstinacy grow. The roots of stinginess, tyranny, and conflict entwine here.

Yet the toilet need not be a battleground. Each sapling differs - some thrive on structure, others rebel against control. Discern the temperament, encourage with care. Share cheerful tales of potties when signs of readiness appear. Move gently, respecting the sacred unfolding of spirit.

Childhood's days are but a handful. Guide with wisdom, not rigid ways, that innate potential may blossom unmarred by fear's barren soil. A garden of acceptance nourishes human flowers to fullest bloom. Tend the ripening soul, that future's orchard may bear sweet fruit.

The Magic of Play for a Child's Growth

Toys are tools for cultivating young minds. Babies first play with fingers and toes, then grasp rattles, entranced by colors and sounds. Keep it simple - one toy at a time, to avoid confusion. When interest wanes, switch to another, enabling full absorption.

Permit children to guide play freely. Dictating what or how squelches enjoyment and learning. Remember, play is their paramount work. Halting a child disrupts their flow and inner release.

Violent toys distort innocence. Through play, fundamentals of life take root. When immersed in healthy play, inner tranquility grows. When deprived, anger and defiance may arise. Foster their joy and curiosity.

Why Children Fib

Lies alarm parents, fearing moral laxity, disasters or external hazards from inadequate supervision. But take care not to overreact. Small untruths are often told to avoid disappointing others.

Rather than condemn, understand fibbing as a passing developmental phase. Guide gently towards honesty through modeling integrity. Meanwhile, appreciate how imagination colors their still forming perception.

Recording and Replaying Reality

Like a budding filmmaker, children silently observe and absorb all around them. Gradually conversations make sense, symbols cohere into representations. Around four, possessions gain value. Praise their constructions, don't arbitrarily discard cherished toys. Provide a play phone to mimic adult roles.

Play together - sharing friendship and guidance. Peers teach much that parents cannot. Nurture interests through exposure and example, not commands. Aid their work of making sense of this vast perplexing world.

The Blessing and Challenge of a Second Child

Consider timing carefully when planning another baby - optimally between three to four years after the first. Gently ask if they would enjoy a sibling. Though initially pleased, adjustment post-birth can prove difficult.

Realize a newborn multiplies, not just adds, work. Attending their needs amidst existing demands strains all. Seek occasional help from the older child but don't overburden.

Suddenly their place feels jeopardized. Reassure them through stories - a lifelong playmate is arriving! Others have adjusted, found joy. This change affects not just them. Listen to their feelings, show extra affection, to weather this transition.

Accustomed to complete attention, now a weak rival seems to have conquered their kingdom! Resistance is natural - briefly regressing to babyish behavior conveys their need for nurturing. Lovingly respond, «You're becoming big and strong like them.» Criticizing their longing for reassurance may stifle maturation.

Studies show single children tend towards more self-focus and social disconnect. Siblings teach cooperation and sharing. Firstborns model maturity for later arrivals, garnering greater acclaim for each milestone achieved. Yet birth order must not dictate limiting roles - each child's spirit longs to soar.

While challenged, firstborns gain immeasurable gifts - empathizing with another's needs, guiding little footsteps. Respect sensitivities but frame the newcomer warmly. Siblings that grow as comrades, not rivals, share life's adventure. Therein may unfold understanding surpassing that imparted by any parents.

The firstborn tends toward solemn duty, while later-borns lean toward carefree abandon, unfettered by expectations. Middle children in a trinity suffer benign neglect, overshadowed between driven eldest and doted-upon youngest. In abundant broods, scarce parental attention breeds insecure sociability.

Around the tender age of three, imagination blossoms, conjuring worlds aligning with inner wants when outer realities disappoint. The self coalesces, integrating varied threads into a coherent tapestry.

Defining intelligence's contours proves slippery. Does it signify adaptability in navigating novel trials? Memory furnishes raw material, while exposure expands the mind's palette. Immerse young spirits in nature's splendor and mankind's diverse creations.

By seven, the body dutifully obeys the mind's intent, thoughts rendered kinetic through willed movement. Yet many stumble in plumbing their emotional depths, unable to decode the nuances of their inner weather. The self-aware have learned to harvest insights from their lush interior landscapes.

Childhood abounds in horizons both endless and fleeting. Tend each budding soul, nourishing uniqueness with wisdom's rains. Seek not rigid conformity but gentle cultivation, that their flourishing branches may in time offer shelter and nourishment to all.

The Gift of Verbal Intelligence

Some remain oblivious to their mind's currents, unable to articulate the silent stream within. Their expression falters, written words eluding capture. The verbally gifted revel in language itself - teaching, storytelling, debating. A ready book or stimulating dialogue is their element. Through honing articulation they better know themselves.

Appreciating Logical, Spatial, and Interpersonal Intelligences

Some possess keen precision with numbers, volumes, and calculations. They grasp relationships between shapes, dimensions, and quantities. Building and engineering come naturally by recognizing affordances in objects.

Others exhibit interpersonal intelligence - able to adopt different perspectives and infer unspoken moods. Navigating social contexts and intuiting needs makes them effective collaborators.

Those gifted with spatial intelligence accurately estimate distances and manipulate mental imagery. They rarely get lost. Even their dreams and fantasies contain vivid graphic elements. Spatial thinking enables fluency with designs, diagrams, and artistic composition.

Multiple aptitudes shine in each child. Identify their special strengths early, then provide the resources to let potentials unfold. Guide them towards fields matching their innate talents. Yet present diverse subjects, lest any domain remains terra incognita. Well-roundedness brews creativity and cross-pollination where singular focus breeds blindness.

Appreciating Nature-Oriented, Artistic, and Social Intelligences

Those gifted with natural intelligence keenly perceive living things - attuned to nature's subtle rhythms and glories. The world is their endless fascination and delight. Kindness, aesthetics, and creativity come naturally to these sensitive souls.

Around five, children become more socially aware. Eager to make their mark, they notice differences between themselves and others. Once set on a positive or negative trajectory, patterns strengthen over time.

Between three and seven, moods evolve every six months. At three-and-a-half, limitless energy and curiosity rule. Play is vital, though still clinging to parents. Around four, imagination blossoms - roleplaying familiar roles. By four-and-a-half, confidence grows as reality focus increases.

Peer interaction is now essential, cooperation blooms but competition arises too. Through alternating cycles of expansion and retreat, the young spirit matures. As social bonds deepen, inner steadiness and empathy have space to grow as well. Our task is to nurture emotional and social intelligence with unwavering compassion.

The Oscillating Moods of Childhood

Comparison breeds envy and disdain. In play, encourage effort, not dominance, lest life become a bitter contest. Around four, cooperative play arises, though each still rules their own realm. Soon, respect for boundaries emerges. Rebellion simmers as self-control is learned - tantrums, defiance, testing limits. Channel this stormy energy with patience.

Five ushers in social rebirth - empathy dawns. Imitating parents, the child yearns to assimilate mature roles. Seize this chance to instill etiquette and self-reflection, yet never shame publicly. Leadership and creativity blossom amidst deepening bonds.

By five-and-a-half, tranquility recedes. Rebelliousness resurges, cooperation vanishes, vulgarity appears. Impossible demands exasperate all. Undercurrents of anger churn beneath this moody surface.

Yet the tempest will pass. Each phase necessitates unique responses to shape character yet avoid recrimination. Discern what the child's behavior signifies rather than just reacting. Meet them where they are, not where we wish them to be. With insight into these oscillations, we gain perspective enabling wiser guidance.

Childhood's terrain is mutable yet fleeting. Traverse its hills and valleys together. Soon the years smooth unpredictable ups and downs into the landscape of maturity. Keep children's essential goodness always in view through the fogs of tumultuous transition.

The Tempests and Tranquility of Six to Eight Years Old

Six ushers in serenity - an optimal time for imparting skills like sports, music, arts matching their interests. Insatiable curiosity compels relentless questioning.

Around seven, turmoil resurges. Children feel inadequate, adrift amidst imagined slights. They crave escape to idealized lives. Rebellion simmers. Yet this storm soon passes.

Parents must understand such oscillations as normal, albeit frustrating, phases. With empathy and consistency, they will ride out these cycles.

Four-year-olds revel in make-believe - dolls, fantasies reveal blossoming creativity. But violent games that glorify destruction should be avoided. Impressionable minds absorb problematic values from such play. Guide them toward activities fostering cooperation, problem-solving and compassion.

When four years old, a child's sense of ownership awakens powerfully regarding parental affection. The beloved mother and father are perceived as exclusively theirs. New infants unleash profound jealousy, as the child's monopoly on parental love becomes shattered. They suffer deeply as attention shifts, feeling forsaken amidst once cherished toys now discarded and forgotten.

Such psychical turmoil in the young soul's tender genesis leaves indelible scars. Lasting damage to the emerging self is inflicted when formative developmental needs go unmet and emotional nourishment is withdrawn. In such conditions, seeds of lasting insecurity, volatility, and inner turmoil take root.

Those deprived of maternal nurturing early on internalize anger and conflict that distorts their natures. Some in adulthood compulsively seek partners compensating for these voids, yet unable to satisfy deeper emotional lacks stemming from childhood's unfulfilled needs, especially the unconditional love of mother. They grow captive to inner demons born of youthful deficits that no lover can remedy.

Between four and five, rudimentary math and reading readiness emerges. Simple counting, shapes, days and seasons - the mind thirsts for patterns and order. Slowly introduce letters, numbers, starting with familiar terms and building systematically.

Curiosity combusts through ceaseless questioning - why is the sky blue? How do batteries work? Patiently engage their probing, nourishing an inquisitive spirit. Have them memorize uplifting poems, addresses, anything bolstering memory and confidence.

If misbehavior arises, redirect calmly before reacting punitively. Reward good behavior consistently with small prizes, fostering self-motivation. Some advocate money to teach economic exchange. Yet be cautious children do not perceive relationships as transactional.

Some psychologists propose using star charts where good behavior earns stars and misdeeds lose them. Children will then strive to fill their chart with stars in order to obtain the consequent reward. This method can instill organization and cooperation as habits in the young child. We can also weave stories for children emphasizing that everyone has a social duty and role to play in society - from baker to doctor to driver - and that all must work diligently and receive wages or points accordingly.

Regarding discipline, it should be considered that the child must be reprimanded at the very moment of committing an inappropriate act, not afterwards by saying we will deal with this when we get home. Nor should a child be punished the next day for something done the previous day. And the child should never be disciplined publicly in front of others.

Some mothers delegate punishment to the fathers. Threatening the child by saying «Just wait until your father gets home, I'll tell him what you did...» conveys to the child that the mother is powerless and weak, while the father is strong and scary. When the mother reports to the father, the child thinks the mother is a tattletale and liar. This turns the beloved father into a harsh disciplinarian, causing him to become angry. Even if the mother does not report to the father, the child still thinks she is dishonest and duplicitous.

There should only be one consistent authority figure, either mother or father. It must be remembered that mistakes happen in all of us all the time. One must be fair and recognize the child does not yet have a proper understanding of right and wrong when committing errors. Allowing healthy freedom and autonomy during childhood is very important. If we constantly impose dos and don'ts in a rigid manner, we will raise dependent beings conditioned to be followers. The objective should be cultivating wisdom and accountability, not mere submission.

Chapter Two
The Healing Elixir of Storytelling

Harnessing Narrative for Transformation

Opening

Stories dwell as luminous gems within the caverns of the psyche, awaiting one holding the mystic lamp of imagination to bring radiance to deep places long shrouded in shadow. In this chapter, we will explore the profound gifts of narrative to transport, illuminate, elevate and mend, like a sage ministering elixirs that restore wholeness to ailing parts.

Storytelling blooms as an ancient healing art passed reverently from generation to generation. Its power springs from deep roots intertwining human experience into a common tapestry, such that we recognize ourselves in fictional guises. In the section «Who Can Conduct Storytherapy,» we consider the blending of technical mastery, intuitive wisdom, and abiding compassion required of consummate storytelling healers. Their role is akin to the alchemist, blending narrative elements into curative draughts.

«The Healing Magic of Storytelling Therapy» reveals how metaphor and reframing limiting tales can empower growth, much as the Traveler's parables enable comprehending oneself from stirring new vantages. Carefully crafted stories externalize inner turmoil, offering cathartic release while unveiling alternate routes ahead.

«The Storytelling Healer - Artist, Scientist and Guide» reflects on how master healers channel arcane wisdom, rigorously assessing impacts, blending psychological insight and creative intuition like the mystic scientist. In «Literature's Power to Heal and Enlighten,» we find stories' gifts to transmute awareness from the leaden slumber of habits into the golden realm of meaning.

«Strategies for Therapeutic Storytelling» offers ways to reshape constricting narratives into heroic quests, dispelling inner demons through allegory's light. Group sharing fosters participation for once-shy souls. We explore storytelling's power to unravel psychological knots and guide children on the quest to author their lives anew.

Thus through storytelling's magic the mind travels unbounded across reality's levels, inhabiting tales that unveil hidden truths. By rewriting the narratives that bind us, we forge purposes aligned with our essence. For within each child an innocent spirit dwells, needing but light and warmth to unfurl its full beauty.

Some enter life imperfect, while others become broken along the way. Certain deficits are obvious from the outset, while others require meticulous discernment to unearth. Science now affords means of diagnosing and even redressing many conditions once deemed immutable. For instance, though autism remains largely intractable, early identification enables ameliorating numerous developmental disabilities.

A child born underweight at nine months, or unresponsive to stimuli, warrants immediate steps to restore vitality. With devoted interventions, many cognitive delays now prove treatable, dramatically enhancing quality of life. But each case deserves unique consideration - there exist no panaceas, only nuanced, compassionate cultivation of every child's inherent potential.

Who Can Conduct Storytherapy?

Storytelling's power to heal springs from deep roots. The storyteller must supremely hone narrative craft, imbuing tales with transformative resonance. A keen intuitive sense for where hidden snarls knot the human spirit comes coupled with wisdom to gently unbind self-imposed constraints. Through cathartic reframing of limiting life narratives, fresh possibilities take shape.

Yet technical mastery alone does not suffice. The heart must hold profound faith in each being's latent wholeness and inherent worth. When bountiful love nourishes our growth, we bloom in turn for one another, blossoming into our most beautiful expressions. Then every life-giving deed and word disperses seeds that will proliferate beyond imagining.

The Healing Magic of Storytelling Therapy

Storytelling therapy entails crafting an absorbing narrative that transforms the listener's inner landscape. The tale's hero models breaking free of limiting mindsets and outdated beliefs. Thereby the client glimpses fresh possibilities for re-authoring their own life story.

The masterful storyteller weaves metaphors that illuminate the client's conflicts and obstacles from new angles. Thereby imagination is awakened to envision alternate routes forward, drawing from inner resources. For the mind can travel untethered through time and space, inhabiting alternate realities that unveil hidden truths. Our unique gift is conceiving that which does not yet exist.

Thus the story becomes the vessel for liberation. The teller must convey hope subtly yet compellingly, allowing the client to identify with the protagonist's liberation while maintaining psychological safety. Through glimpsing a similar situation in fictional guise, enlightening insights dawn, linking disparate episodes into a coherent realization.

The skillful therapist thereby guides the client in externalizing and reframing their troubles as a detached narrative. Perspective expands on the broader context behind behaviors and choices. Creative listening allows the client's authentic needs and desires to emerge. Insight blossoms by making the unconscious conscious through the alchemy of narrative.

For when we illuminate the shadows with compassion, imaginary demons shrink and dissolve, dispelled by courage and self-understanding. The client thus transforms from passive victim to active author, empowered to edit their life-story and script new chapters. Our calling is igniting this agency, that their true selves may finally flourish.

The Storytelling Healer – Artist, Scientist and Guide

The masterful storytelling healer is part artist, part scientist - blending human insight with rigorous methodology. Like an investigative journalist, they carefully document each session's process and impacts. Psychological knowledge informs their work, yet technical expertise alone does not suffice. For head must harmonize with heart for lasting remediation to occur.

Thus the consummate healer is also part shaman - channeling mysterious wisdom from realms beyond the rational. With care, creativity and compassion, they midwife the client's self-actualization. Through immersive narrative, they stimulate psychological knots to unwind, opening space for breakthroughs.

Above all, an unwavering faith in our intrinsic wholeness motivates their endeavor. They walk alongside each struggling soul until liberation is achieved. By publishing discoveries, they advance the healing arts for all. For knowledge bereft of compassion is sterile, while compassion alone remains powerless to combat suffering at scale. The healer integrally blends insight, imagination and care - modeling our human potential fully realized.

Literature's Power to Heal and Enlighten

Great writing penetrates the soul, stirring insight and imagination. Narrative transports us, revealing life's possibilities. Storytelling forges profound connection through shared vulnerability and meaning.

Beyond therapy, literature broadly educates the human spirit. Folk tales convey cross-cultural, national and homeland wisdom, modeling courage and morality. Relatable characters mirror our struggles, tracing the path from confusion to purpose. We identify with their quest for self-knowledge, traveling alongside towards truth.

Stories unveil society's injustices, kindling the urge to remedy suffering. They compel moral clarity, moving us beyond complacency. Though darkness may gather, redemption ever remains possible.

Literature reflects our longing for belonging. We take heart knowing our trials are universal, our dreams unified. Tales tap the wellsprings of emotion, at once entertaining, uplifting and cathartic. They prompt reappraisal of assumptions worn rigid by habit, opening windows to breathe fresh perspective.

For at its best, literature speaks to the timeless essence within us all. It is the song of humanity reverberating through the ages, chronicling our eternal striving. When eloquence marries insight, words wield the power to awaken, heal and transform.

Strategies for Therapeutic Storytelling With Challenged Children

When telling stories therapeutically, first choose simple, uplifting tales to build trust and engagement. Then gradually interweave metaphorical dilemmas needing resolution. Thereby the child's coping abilities and perceptual filters emerge.

Has harsh labeling warped their self-concept - stupid, weird, lazy? Reframing limiting narratives is vital. Have protagonists model self-confidence and resilience. Externalize inner demons through allegorical enemies to be conquered.

Ask insightful questions prompting introspection. How do you define failure, or beauty? What exemplifies courage to you? Avoid abstract analysis by portraying dynamics through relatable characters. Thereby maladaptive thought patterns surface while seeds of liberation take root.

With rapport established, introduce thornier scenarios requiring growth. Portray setbacks and injustices, yet highlight perseverance and redemption. The child learns adversity can be overcome by inner resolve, not fate. Slowly expand the narrative's complexity as capabilities mature.

By discussing stories, children externalize and objectify personal struggles. Once embodied in a protagonist, painful issues become less threatening. Compassionate listening and mirroring build insight, point by point enlarging their circle of compassion. Storytelling mentors the young in humanity's ancient wisdom while kindling their unique creative spark.

Thus we nurture budding wholeness. Where brokenness once shadowed, now stand repaired and open vistas. For within each child dwells an innocent spirit needing but light and warmth to bloom in its fullness.

The masterful storyteller reframes the tale to illuminate the heroic within the broken. Where the child feels doomed by fate, possibilities are unveiled. Each life contains untapped wells of motivation and meaning. By accessing this submerged potency through narrative alchemy, paralyzing traps transform into growth opportunities.

The healer carefully monitors which metaphors produce shifts in perspective. For though all experience suffering, each journey traverses unique terrain. Those with purpose invent self-validating narratives, while the aimless remain mystified by events. Thus the storyteller should gently guide the child's gaze towards attainable goals ahead.

Periodically we must look back to integrate the past, making sense of trials endured. How did you survive this ordeal? What new insights emerged? What dreams now spur you onward? By indirectly prompting such questions through allegory, mentors provide way-markers to guide the young along their quest.

For within each child stirs a vitalizing spirit, however obscured by circumstance. Should conditioning smother innate drives, the psyche rebels through subconscious yearnings and unrest. But by honoring authentic inner voices, we foster wisdom over fear, unlocking developmental potentials awaiting activation.

Parents and society erect schemas of prohibition and shame which shape emerging identity. Children Learn to split the speakable from the taboo, burying unresolved shame that continues poisoning the psyche. By encouraging open and non-judgmental dialogue, healers transform broken secrecy into reconciled integrity.

Effective Techniques for Therapeutic Storytelling

In some methods, the client narrates an experience, unconsciously projecting their struggles into the account. The healer then reframes the tale, embodying the central problem as a metaphorical enemy – perhaps a devious animal – who tries but fails to frighten the protagonist.

With each retelling, the menacing creature is further humiliated as the hero's power grows. Thereby the child is empowered to conquer their own inner demons. For quandaries often trace back to distorted memories crystallized into psychological knots. By creatively reconstructing the narrative, the therapist dissolves those sickening barbs.

When recounting painful events, the client's demeanor shifts at moments of hidden trauma. The astute storyteller homes in on these disclosures, gently unraveling the sources of suffering. After summarizing the ordeal, they inquire about overlooked dimensions still haunting the victim.

Then the healer radically recasts the plot - transporting the protagonist into the throes of an epic battle against the very powers formerly vanquishing them. But this time, they emerge triumphant, armed with newly forged strengths and realizations. Thereby the client rehearses victory over once-undefeated inner tyrants.

Our lives' meanings derive not from events themselves, but the narratives we construct from selective memory. By rewriting stories that bind us, we unwind old chains and forge liberating new purposes. For creativity arises from migrating across levels of reality. From the interplay of darkness and light, inspiration sparks and characters morph, spawning insight.

Pitfalls to Avoid

Enliven the narrative through dramatic gestures and vocal modulation attuned to each moment.

Ensure the story aligns with the child's age and interests to maximize engagement.

Maintain eye contact to sustain an empathetic connection throughout the telling.

Modulate the pace to match the child's comprehension level so the tale remains gripping yet coherent.

Speak clearly in a compelling yet warm tone that complements the emotional journey.

Draw the child into collaboratively telling a shared story, taking turns and building on each other's contributions.

Gently prompt them to articulate anxieties through having characters externalize emotions.

For disabled children, respectfully incorporate those realities into stories where protagonists model resilience and capability despite challenges. Invite them to co-create such empowering narratives.

The storyteller's art entails inhabiting multiple perspectives and planes of consciousness. By modeling sensitivity, creativity and courage, mentors unpack insights that restore wholeness and wonder to worlds where suffering once shadowed.

For our words to heal others requires honing both narrative artistry and profound human insight. Masterful delivery must marry a compassionate purpose. Stories succeed when audiences recognize truth in fictional guises. When teller, tale and listener sync, transformation unfolds.

Effective Characterization and Plot Development in Therapeutic Storytelling

Characters may be animals, objects or imaginary beings tailored to the child's interests. Benevolent sages can voice disguised insights -an owl dispensing wisdom, say. Abstract teachings emerge indirectly when protagonists consult these guides at pivotal moments. Thereby suppressed emotions surface as the child identifies with imaginary proxies.

Occasionally pause and ask the child to recap, ensuring active engagement. Vary techniques to sustain dynamism - dramatizing with puppets or music, incorporating participatory elements and sensory details. Most crucially, craft a compelling plot eliciting their investment and anticipation.

In group settings, gently coax shy members into contributing by assigning roles. Integrate verbal storytelling with expressive arts like illustrating key scenes to reinforce messages visually.

The process unfolds gradually:

First, building trust. Then planning appropriate narratives and imagery aimed at catharsis. Next, activating imagination to trace alternative trajectories. Thereafter, releasing suppressed anxieties embodied in the characters. Finally, reflecting on insights gained and integrating breakthroughs into everyday life.

For within each child dwells a seed of wisdom and creativity awaiting nurturing. By offering empathy, fellow-feeling and inspiration, mentors help scatter inhibitions so those latent potentials may unfold.

Assessing Individual Needs and Tailoring the Therapeutic Approach

Storytelling therapy aims to transform limiting beliefs and bolster positive self-concepts, especially for children prone to pessimism. The negativity bias surfaces in those fixating on threats and misfortunes. More resilient children also acknowledge adversity yet emphasize overcoming hardship.

Therapeutic storytelling can be conducted one-on-one or in groups. Individually, the storyteller hooks interest in an unfolding drama then lets the child continue the narrative. In groups, members collectively improvise unfinished tales, taking turns elaborating on the plot.

Participatory elements like chanting rhythmic poems build collective joy. Call-and-response exchanges reinforce lessons while energizing shy participants. Such techniques can benefit all ages, ameliorating mood disorders, developmental delays, trauma, disabilities, depression and more. Group settings foster peer bonding and self-esteem, yet individual attention remains essential to address unique needs.

First observe thought patterns – are negative assumptions distorting the child's self-concept? Then craft stories targeting cognitive distortions and modeling self-efficacy. Reshape perspectives from pessimism towards realistic optimism. Or simply allow creativity's spark through arts, music and communality. For inherent resilience flourishes when children feel heard, valued and part of a compassionate community.

Healing arises through discovering mirrors in fiction - recognizing shared struggles dressed in metaphor's guise. By opening closed systems of isolation, energy circulates to nourish barren branches. Cradled by care, our essential goodness unfurls.

Various Disabilities

There are all different kinds of disabilities and dysfunctions, each can be addressed and treated with care and wisdom. Below most critical ones with the proper storytelling techniques are highlighted.

Children With Cognitive Disabilities

The degree of intellectual disability determines appropriate interventions. Some comprehend basic narrative and benefit from enriched engagement fostering focus, coordination, emotional regulation and thinking skills.

How to Tell Stories for This Group

Simple vocabulary and gestural dramatization aid comprehension. The child may also act out portions of the story. Embedding behavioral modeling into dramatic scenarios indirectly imparts pragmatic life skills. Finding apt words to express their situation builds linguistic capacity.

Rewarding progress, however incremental, boosts morale essential for growth. Improvisational storytelling allows tailoring narratives to each child's cognitive level and social development stage. Keep sentences concise given limited working memory. Rhythmic poems and music aid retention and enjoyment.

Above all, remain patient and celebrate every hard-won victory. For our faith in those dismissed by the world kindles embers within the spirit to persevere through daunting odds. In time, personal strengths crystallize that others overlook.

Children With Learning Delays

Children hindered in their learning, while not outright deficient, face obstacles in concentration, cognition, speech, literacy, pronunciation, and overall comprehension. Unable to keep pace with peers, these youths struggle in executing mathematical operations. The root causes are varied: disorder in key mental processes, disabilities from brain injury, or congenital neurological conditions. Some endure visual or auditory impairments, or speak incomprehensibly. Most cannot read aloud nor grasp the meaning of texts. They lack facility in discerning distances, time, and spatial relationships. Directions and quantities confound them. Certain of these children are restless in behavior, incapable of tracing a straight line. Their memory fails to retain lessons, lacking conception of amounts, dimensions, bearings, or intervals.

Storytelling for Children With Learning Delays

The art of storytelling for children with learning delays must begin with an opening question, priming young minds for the unfolding narrative. Employ theatrical gestures and poses to bring the tale to life. Maintain steady eye contact, amusing with wry expressions to elicit smiles. Thus will the child discover an easier comprehension. Group story therapy proves ideal if feasible.

In a group setting, invite collective responses to the story's prompts. Rhythmic, succinct tales work best. Use simple, familiar words suiting the group's vocabulary. As the child cannot yet sketch a straight line, have them connect dots penciled on paper as a game. Animal sounds and nature, plus painted imagery, will heighten their incentive to listen. Music serves to effectively capture their attention.

Regular physical touch grounds the child's focus. Rewarding is also essential; praise, prizes and treats motivate. At times raise your voice suddenly to reclaim wandering thoughts. Experience shows that the therapist's warmth and empathy play a pivotal role. Allow time for concepts to solidify in the child's mind, repeating if necessary. Enable the child to engage with the themes; imagine themselves the brave, striving protagonist, instilling a sense of heroic potential.

A story must follow a single thread, else the child grows confused, unable to concurrently ponder two plots. Yet their listening and expressive skills will gradually refine. The storyteller must recognize that the patient discerns slowly, struggles with their own body and surroundings. Writing, math, and symbols challenge them; abundant patience and time are requisites. Read a book aloud, then recapitulate and depict it to re-engage attention. Stress that this is not illness but correctable behavior.

Prognostication proves highly effective for such children. Remarkably, their comprehension and capabilities expand through story therapy. Concentration increases, retention of text improves, and even their sense of heroism and self-belief strengthens. Learning multiplication tables rhythmically, for example, can benefit mental calculations.

The storyteller's art minimizes distractibility. Experience shows that their benevolence and steadiness plays a major role in rousing the child's learning and activity.

Selective Mutism

Selective mutism, of the anxiety disorder breed, arises by the patient's own election. The child, entering social exchange, declines to initiate conversation or answer queries. This reticence afflicts adults and children alike. At home they may chatter unhindered, yet fall mute at school, thus avoiding attendance and inviting academic troubles. Excessive shyness and fear of public exposure further characterize the disorder. Withdrawal, seclusion, even subtle rebellion or defiance also manifest mildly.

Diagnosing Selective Mutism Involves:

1. Persistent inability to converse in expected social situations like school, hampering educational, vocational or social advancement.

2. Incapacity for social speech unrelated to unawareness of conversational norms.

This rare condition typically emerges before age five, often going unnoticed until schooling exposes greater social detachment. Common outcomes include severe deterioration in academic or social functioning, and mockery or harassment from classmates.

How to Tell Stories to Children With Selective Mutism

Shaping techniques aid treating selective mutism, gently coaxing the child to speak. First, nonverbal engagement earns reinforcing prompts. Then rewards follow vocalizing certain sounds, like animal noises or alphabet letters. Next, single words merit prizes, progressively building verbal facility. Psychologists concur that pharmaceutical remedies also benefit selective mutism.

Autistic Children:

These youths find comfort in simplicity, resisting any change of surroundings. Speech emerges involuntarily. Basic playthings occupy them in listless, aimless repetition. None display the high-spirited mischief expected in their peers. Bewilderment prevails, though outwardly typical. Despite unimpaired faculties, they cannot connect with others their age, nor people in general. Some remain mute. They entertain themselves monotonously with habitual toys, devoid of intent or motivation. Such absence of playfulness is a hallmark, as is improper pronoun use, saying «you are hungry» instead of «I am hungry.»

When offered an item, indifference meets the gesture. Seeking their attention proves futile, eye contact unforthcoming. Only hunger, thirst or discomfort prompts approaching their parents. Some exhibit the opposite extreme, clinging to mother and resisting separation. Endless repetitive questioning - «what day is it today?», «what time is it now?» - tries the patience of loved ones. With limited vocabulary, comprehension falters. Misused pronouns like «you are hungry» reveal linguistic challenges.

How to Tell Stories to Autistic Children

Storytelling proves challenging with such detached youths. They spurn social connection, evading the storyteller's overtures. Some remain silent; others repeat phrases compulsively. Many mimic sounds, so imitation assists in engaging them. Remarkably, some exhibit uncanny gifts for music or art. Their keen observation translates into exquisitely detailed drawings. Others display prodigious musical talent. Some astonish with their flawless recall, computing like machines. Given a phonebook, they memorize all the numbers; asked the day of a date decades past, they unfailingly respond - yet cannot add simple sums. This savant syndrome likely owes to genetic inheritance, though no medical remedy exists presently.

Still, creativity and patience may penetrate their inner realm. As characters mirror the child's talents, storylines validate their experiences. Surprise elements grab attention while rhythmic language and repeated refrains aid retention. The storyteller's tone should remain low, warm and soothing. Visual aids like puppets and props add tactile interest. Most importantly, these sensitive children must retain control; the story follows their cues.

When they feel heard and accepted, a bridge extends to their isolated island. Through empathic tales, they discover the joys of sharing, slowly emerging to connect with the wider world.

Children With Speech or Comprehension Disorders

Afflicted youths stutter or cannot vocalize at all, lacking orderly expression. Certain words prove difficult, with hesitations between terms, hence impeding development compared to peers. Sometimes blame lies with cerebral palsy, brain damage from past trauma, or birth injury. In any case, the child feels engulfed in crisis, acting out in compensation for frustrations. Since they cannot keep pace, others bear scolding. Withdrawal and fantasy offer escape. Behavior seems more childish than classmates. Destructive release brings some relief.

Inarticulate children, hampered by localized brain lesions, struggle to communicate verbally. Physical deformities like cleft palate can also disrupt air passage through the nose and mouth. Cerebral palsy arises when the motor control center of the brain malfunctions.

How to Tell stories to Children With Speech and Comprehension Disorders

First gain trust through affection, accepting rather than chastising outbursts. Offer embraces, caresses - understand their limits, then commence the tale.

Craft stories bolstering self-worth, negating violent urges, alleviating apprehension. Let the hero lead from inward focus to beautiful aspirations. Complement narration with art, music or pantomime avoiding verbal demands. Provide technical training in scene staging for imagined situations.

Act out riding an imaginary boat amidst crashing rain, thunder and lightning, rising waves, tension and near drowning, until sudden rescue. Through sounds, lighting and miming each moment - portraying mounting panic, inviting participation - the child feels immersed in the peril. Gradually their engagement intensifies. Such peaks and valleys awaken their mind.

The storyteller must tune into each unique child, following their cues to foster expression. Repetition aids comprehension and retention, as do exaggerated vocal tones and gestures. Most importantly, shower the child with encouragement to develop confidence. A little imagination reveals their limitless inner riches.

Children With Personality Disorders

Such troubled youths suffer distorted self-identity, unable to engage reality. Comprehension falters, immersing them in ceaseless dread and delusion. Maturation lags, deviant personal and social conduct emerges. Transgression tantalizes, disordered thinking swerves into raving.

Impaired cognition breeds aggression, rupturing bonds.

Flawed discernment summons delusions.

Defective emotions induce apathy.

Disturbed self-awareness creates an existential crisis.

Weakened volition saps motivation and interest.

Deranged psyche and movement prompt bizarre behavior, hyperactivity or lethargy.

For these children, stories must tread sensitively, indirectly revealing a healthier path. As fictional characters overcome similar troubles, the child feels understood, not judged. Symbolic plot points provide perspective on distorted thinking.

How to Tell Stories to Children With Personality Disorders

Storytelling for such patients requires utmost care and prudence. As their state shifts unpredictably, the storyteller must adapt accordingly, given complicating personal traits.

Under a psychiatrist's guidance, narrative activities ought to judiciously cultivate awareness and mental engagement. Learning vocabulary and proper enunciation enables connecting through role-play.

Gradually the tale guides the child through peaks and valleys, depicting such turbulence as a shared human experience, survived by all. A fresh perspective and coping methods are presented. The account lifts their sense of collapse with hope. Group storytelling proves ideal if feasible, airing each child's memories and anecdotes to stimulate collective participation. Posing questions, having them act out characters, further engages attention and interest.

Meanwhile, upbeat music and a welcoming ambience reinforce therapeutic gains. For milder cases, fictional heroes model perseverance through adversity, alleviating the child's own anxieties. Interactive elements empower self-expression.

Hyperactive Children

Such restless youths remain ever in motion, scarcely contained in one place. Ceaseless activity and agitation prevail. Each moment brings new movements and noise, with abrupt, jerky gestures. Heedlessness hinders learning, despite intact cognition. They cannot attend to others' words or organize themselves.

This disorder affects more boys than girls, as if their spirit overflows its vessel. Forced stillness only relocates the commotion to jiggling limbs. Though mentally sound, inattentiveness impedes scholastics. Not just the body, but the mind too races repetitively. Anxieties sometimes arise, relieved when the turbulence subsides.

A severe form manifests in childhood mania, harboring depressive potential afterwards. Some experts in fact consider hyperactivity an expression of depression. In adults this emerges as exhaustion, while exuberant restlessness marks it in youth.

Children with attention deficits misplace belongings, distraction invading even direct conversation. Failing to queue orderly, they respond without thinking. Chatter and disruption thrive. No classmate escapes their radius of disruption. Highly sensitive to noise, they seek imaginative escapes, blinking repeatedly, talking to themselves.

How to Tell Stories to Hyperactive Children

Storytelling for such restless souls requires great patience and creativity. The narrator must adapt to the child's incessant fluctuations, attending their swirling thoughts and emotions.

The story itself should incorporate frequent changes to align with their limited attention span. Lengthy plots lose them; they readily abandon the tale halfway. Puzzles, music and art making can run alongside the narrative to hold interest. Dramatizing motions and gestures also proves effective. One strategy involves joining the child's play and continuing the story within their game.

Children With Speech and Comprehension Disorders

Such children either cannot speak fluently or fail to articulate words. They may disregard proper sentence structure, vocalizing with difficulty. Speech delay indicates stunted development compared to peers. Dysarthria stems from localized brain damage, garbling verbal communication. Cleft palate causes air passage disorders. Cerebral palsy implies impaired movement control centers.

Core challenges include comprehending language, and wielding speech to convey ideas, needs and opinions. Frustrations over their thwarted interactions prompt frequent outbursts.

Some retreat into seclusion and fantasy; others regress to more childish manners. Destructive release offers recompense for these deficiencies.

How to Tell Stories to Children With Speech and Comprehension Disorders

Through nurturing tales, the storyteller bolsters the child's confidence. Reading aloud, then inviting them to vocalize rhythmic sounds or sing simple melodies, provides gentle practice without judgment. Offer steady encouragement to strengthen proper enunciation, vocabulary, sentences and articulation. Patiently allow the child to unload frustrations over their incapacities.

Ask them to recount stories, mimic sounds, express emotions. Reward each effort. Assist with pronounciation or word retrieval without excessive correction.

Deaf Children

Deaf children relish visual stimulation, approaching the world inquisitively, though frustration and isolation may arise from communication barriers. Some benefit from hearing aids, while others remain unable to hear.

How to Tell Stories to Deaf Children

The storyteller requires skill in lip reading and sign language to connect. Blend narrative with drawing, miming expressively, displaying vivid nature photos and gestures of animal kindness. Dramatize amusing, bizarre events through role-play. Share excitement by facial expressions and gestures.

Such multi-sensory methods captivate the child's engagement, forging bonds with the empathic storyteller. Add story transcripts to aid comprehension. Incorporate signs representing key actions and emotions.

Children With Severe Physical Illnesses

Youth gravely afflicted with immobility face profound challenges. Paralysis, cancer, multiple sclerosis and similar traumas constrain them. Bedridden children especially struggle as their development demands play and activity. Pain pervades their world until the storyteller's visit offers respite.

How to Tell Stories to Children With Severe Physical Illnesses

Fantastical, joyful tales can illuminate the bleak sickbed, especially when accompanied by uplifting music to dispel isolation and gloom. Anxiety yields to narratives providing solace. Even the despondent, pained or depressed may find escape in an engaging story.

Prolonged immobility often disheartens the spirit. In such cases, infuse stories with auspicious tidings to kindle recovery's spark. Bookish children derive comfort from vivid volumes on flying machines and soaring themes. Nature's beauty in photos, cheerful melodies and hopeful art lift the child's essence from weary confinement into imaginative flight.

Blind Children

Unlike cognitive disabilities, blindness relates not to intellect. Deprived of sight, their other senses thrive - touch, hearing, smell. Memory excels through necessity, learning ability persists undiminished.

How to Tell Stories to Blind Children

Nature themes resonate deeply for these youths - the storyteller's voice should ring rich and clear, never rushed. Slow pacing risks boredom as their intellect is unimpaired. Weave descriptive passages of rippling streams, raindrops, rustling leaves to transport their keen imagination. Group tales build communal bonds.

Visually impaired children also benefit from reading encouragement to gradually gain proficiency. Provide ample spacing between large printed words and raised images to trace. Surrounding tactile paintings arouse curiosity in tandem with narrative. This boosts confidence, motivating further exploration. Textured storybooks engage their senses wholly. Guiding the child's fingers across embossed shapes can vivify the unfolding tale.

Foul-mouthed or Aggressive Children

Enduring apprehension plagues such youths, quick to assume a defensive or combative stance. Foul language prevails; they reject any viewpoint but their own. Often sexually unrestrained, anxiety constantly churns within. Weak self-image, emotional volatility and poor academics accompany this turmoil. Building trust requires infinite patience.

How to Tell Stories to Foul-mouthed or Aggressive Children

The storyteller must first establish credibility with such youths, demonstrating worldly grit exceeding their own. They equate toughness with power, so the narrator reveals their capacity for hardness, unafraid of ugliness. Yet this posturing merely provides entry to interact.

Wicked Children

Wayward youth often exhibit traits distinguishing their conduct, including inattention, flouting rules, self-loathing, provoking others, and inability to solve problems constructively. Diverse factors may be culpable - upbringing, personality, genetics or psychological conditions. Still, with compassionate guidance, these children can gain self-awareness, outgrowing destructive patterns.

How to Tell Stories to Wicked Children

To tell stories effectively to wicked children, the storyteller must establish a bold, fearless persona by boasting of daring exploits and acting aggressively. This involves spinning exciting tales of harsh exploits and acting aggressively - shouting suddenly, pacing aggressively, boasting of one's own daring deeds, which impresses the child so they view the storyteller as the dominant «alpha», allowing engagement.

Once the child is receptive, the subsequent stories subtly promote positive lessons, as the hero realizes it's better to abide by laws, accommodate society, and respect others' rights, despite their own past transgressions. The message is woven indirectly rather than stated overtly.

Throughout the process the storyteller maintains their tough facade to preserve the child's trust. But the real work happens through compassionate content once the child's defenses are lowered. The hard exterior provides entry to nurture the gentle heart now open to change through empathic storytelling.

Socially Maladjusted Children

Deceitfulness distinguishes such youths, who become adept at lying. Theft and pyromania manifest, with aggressive tendencies. Physical coordination often falters. Irritability and mood swings prevail, anxiety churning within. Insecurity and powerlessness plague their inner world.

Engaging these children demands much energy. They feign accord with the storyteller while anticipating chances to react. Their words lack substance, promises unfulfilled.

How to Tell Stories to Socially Maladjusted Children

Initially, the storyteller must establish credibility by conveying even greater daring. Spinning frightening tales with harsh language simulates the child's mindset, gaining their respect. Once dominant, slowly transition the narratives toward harmony, friendship and unity.

Imparting skills like art or drama facilitates engagement. Technical training blended with storytelling also proves effective. Yet such posturing merely provides entry to interact.

Children Who Bite Their Nails and Fingers

This habit often arises from anxiety, stress, or as an outlet for frustration and distress. Sometimes learned by observing others, it can also signal low self-confidence. Aware it is undesirable, the child may hide their hands around others. If unchecked in youth, the tendency persists into adulthood.

Keep nails trimmed to minimize damage when urges strike. Distract or redirect rather than chastise them, which only worsens matters. The goal is replacing the nervous habit with healthier coping skills over time.

How to Tell Stories to Children Who Bite Their Nails and Fingers

First, identify sources of anxiety by inviting the child to share or depict their worries through storytelling or art. Once underlying issues surface, soothing nature tales build self-assurance and optimism.

Personify each finger with eyes, mouths and voices so they interact as characters. Have them describe their functions and value, boosting appreciation of hands. Assign family/friends' names to fingers to build emotional connection.

Children With Bed-wetting Issues

Though continence often develops around age 4, nighttime accidents persisting to 7 warrant medical consultation. Contributing factors may include:

- Diabetes
- Urinary infections
- Anxiety
- Allergies
- Fears
- New environments
- Parental misconduct
- New sibling
- Bereavement
- Divorce
- Deep sleeping
- Fainting spells
- Hernias
- Genetic predisposition
- Chromosomal abnormalities

Harsh reactions exacerbate matters, hindering improvement. The child dreads travel or sleepovers, fearing humiliation if accidents occur. Never discuss this issue with others, which only amplifies their shame. Instead, bring them to the restroom before bedtime, limit fluids, and awaken half-way through the night for bathroom trips.

How to Tell Stories to Children With Bed-wetting Issues

Stories can rebuild self-esteem damaged by this condition. Tell of others who overcame the same struggle, now happily waking up dry each morning - proof of permanent victory. Reward the child daily for dry nights.

Transgender Children

Signs of transgender identity often emerge in early childhood. Parents may notice preferences for toys, colors, or mannerisms atypical of the child's sex assigned at birth. While subtle or fleeting, these cues may indicate gender discordance, risking dysphoria if unaddressed.

If clearly experiencing disconnect between physical and psychological gender, medical intervention can be cautiously considered, enabling development of secondary sex characteristics aligning with identity. This momentous decision warrants prudence, as effects prove irreversible.

How to Tell Stories to Transgender Children

The narrator sensitively depicts characters mirroring the child's transition, normalizing it as a possible life event. This validation assists embracing their new identity.

If a transgender boy, frame tales around bravery and latent strengths. For a transgender girl, emotional narratives and artistic themes prove affirming. The storyteller plays a vital role in reinforcing the child's emerging self-concept.

These parenting methods diminish children's creativity:

1. Issuing orders and prohibitions

2. Imposing rigid roles on the child

3. Disregarding the child's creations

4. Inflexible, authoritarian rules

5. Instilling fear of failure

6. Unhealthy competitiveness

7. Focusing solely on outcomes rather than process

8. Comparing the child to others

9. Criticizing outcomes harshly

10. Rushing work

11. The mentor's autocratic perspective on outcomes

12. Humiliating the child

13. Demanding too much beyond child's abilities

14. Using violence

15. Excessive attention

16. Satisfying every wish

17. Overindulgence with money

18. Having excessive expectations

19. Over-scheduling classes and activities

20. Unrealistic illusions about the child's abilities

21. Hypocritical behaviors

22. Providing opportunities at inappropriate times

23. Lying

24. Repetitive trips

25. Repetitive foods

26. Taking the same route to school daily

27. Repetitive snacks

28. Repetitive lessons

29. Pointless, tedious instruction

30. Not spending time in nature

31. Being overprotective

32. Lack of diverse recreational activities

33. Disregarding the child's opinions

34. Boring, repetitive weekends without amusement

35. Not introducing books

36. Lack of socialization with others

37. Not answering the child's questions

38. Excessive schoolwork

39. Not discussing family issues with the child

40. Excessive orderliness

41. Prioritizing others' tasks over the child

42. Only child loneliness

43. Not playing with the child

44. Becoming habituated to mundanity

45. Disregarding the child's emotions

46. Home environment discordant with the child's conditions

47. Not allowing the child to freely express themselves

48. Parents' repetitive behaviors and speech

49. Insufficient environmental stimuli for the child

50. Rigid and inflexible parents

51. Hitting the child

52. Parents not keeping up to date and being backwards

53. Excessive cartoon viewing

54. Excessive computer game play

55. Parental obsessiveness

56. Uncreative parents

57. Being overcautious

58. Fear of failure and mistakes

59. Parents' idealistic thinking

60. Mother being away from child for long hours

61. Parents not aligned in child rearing

62. Lack of goals and plans in family life

63. Imposing adult roles prematurely

64. Disregarding the child's imagination

65. Fear of societal judgment

66. Parents overemphasizing gender

67. Lack of access to suitable toys

68. Viewing inappropriate films

69. Overemphasis on grades

70. Parental addiction

71. Using inappropriate nicknames for the child

72. Verbal abuse and swearing

73. No lightheartedness or humor at home

74. Misuse of books, not curating accessible books for the child

75. Poor response to the child's mistakes

76. Lack of parents' self-identity

77. Inattentiveness to the child's questions

78. Inattentiveness to the child's nutrition

79. Rebuking the child without allowing self-defense

80. Depression

Author's Bio

The prolific author Violet Razegh Panah, a writer, poet, painter and researcher, has published extensively since 1994. Her beloved children's books «Stories of Mommy and I» (Two Volumes) were named Book of the Year in 1996 by the Children's Book Council of Iran, among other accolades. These tales became national best-sellers in 1999, while also winning the IBBY Prize at the New Delhi Festival for their imaginative illustrations.

Ms. Razegh Panah's commitment to ideals of peace and tolerance is evidenced in «The Mir Space Station,» awarded First Prize in 2001 by UNESCO for literature serving these universal values. Among 309 writers representing 58 nations, her vision of unity and hope for humanity's future shone bright. Similarly, the book was honored by the Munich Library the same year. Published internationally from India to Malaysia, her books transcend borders.

Her other book «Viva Iran» springs from intimate interviews with contemporary luminaries who have each played a vital role in the cultural enrichment of their homeland. In their own sweetly engaging voices, this book relates the childhood stories of these remarkable individuals, chronicling their early journeys with charm and readability. Through these personal narratives, the reader gains insight into the wellsprings that nourished the greatness within these icons who have meaningfully contributed to the elevation of Iran.

Additional works include «The Third Season», «Call Me», «The World is Mine» (Two Volumes), «The Biography of Mrs. Touran Mirhadi» and «The Wandering Pinkie», with the latter translated into Malay and Javanese. From 1999-2006, she authored research books for Shahid Beheshti University of Iran while pioneering story therapy techniques.

www.ingramcontent.com/pod-product-compliance
Lightning Source LLC
Chambersburg PA
CBHW060339290526
45793CB00003B/667